Reb

Covenant Keepers

Covenant
Keepers

Unlocking the Miracles
God Wants for You

Wendy Watson Nelson

DESERET
BOOK

Salt Lake City, Utah

PHOTO CREDITS

Page 4: Photo courtesy of the author. Page 8: Galyna Andrushko/shutterstock.com.
Page 14: Lisa Thornberg/iStockphoto. Page 21: Terry Wilson/iStockphoto.
Page 27: *Interrupting Angels,* © Annie Henrie Nader, used with permission.
Page 34: PRG-Estudio/iStockphoto. Page 42: pattiz/iStockphoto.
Page 51: Photo courtesy of the author. Page 60: Ejla/iStockphoto.
Page 67: Osugi/shutterstock.com.

Library of Congress Cataloging-in-Publication Data

Nelson, Wendy Watson, 1950–   author.
  Covenant keepers : unlocking the miracles God wants for you / Wendy
Watson Nelson.
      pages cm
  Includes bibliographical references.
  ISBN 978-1-62972-162-0 (hardbound : alk. paper)
1. Christian life—Mormon authors. 2. Covenants—Religious aspects—The
Church of Jesus Christ of Latter-day Saints. 3. The Church of Jesus Christ
of Latter-day Saints—Doctrine. 4. Mormon Church—Doctrine. I. Title.
  BX8656.N443 2016
  248.4'893—dc23   2015034649

Printed in the United States of America
Publishers Printing, Salt Lake City, UT

10   9   8   7   6   5   4   3   2   1

CONTENTS

OUR COVENANTS ARE A GIFT! A gift from God designed to get us safely back Home to Him![1]

What a gift that is![2]

When it comes to making and keeping covenants with God, *nothing* is more important. And *nothing* is more filled with power!

Those were my conclusions after several months of thinking nonstop about covenants in response to an invitation to speak at a BYU Women's Conference.

I had immersed myself in the scriptures; studied the words of prophets, seers, and revelators; and listened more attentively than ever to the words of our baptismal, sacramental, and temple covenants.

I had asked great women and men from various

places around the world—from Preston, England, to Tokyo, Japan—what it means to them that they have made covenants with God.

Further, as I immersed myself in family history research, I felt the unmistakable urgency of those living on the other side of the veil who are desperate to make covenants with God—*now!*

We often refer to ourselves as men and women of covenant or as covenant women and men. But what does that really mean?

One sister expressed it this way: "It means I've promised God that I will follow His Son in what I do, think, and say. And I've made those promises by entering into sacred covenants that bind me to both the Father and the Son."

One brother said: "Covenants are a symbol of my faith and desire to follow the Savior. Remembering that I have made these covenants helps me make better choices in my life."

Elder Jeffrey R. Holland gave the following definition: "A covenant is a binding spiritual contract, a solemn promise to God our Father that we will live and think and act a certain way—the way of His Son, the Lord Jesus Christ. In return, the Father, Son, and Holy Ghost promise us the full splendor of eternal life."[3]

He emphasized that the subject of covenants "is a very personal subject."

So, what does it mean to *you* that you have made covenants with God?

Before we go any further, let's put our focus on covenants within the context of the days in which we live.

People often ask my husband and me: "What's one of your favorite places you've ever visited?"

We typically answer—in unison, "Our backyard! A place we don't get to visit as often as we'd like!"

But seriously, one of my favorite places is Moscow, Russia. Why?

Because of what I experienced there within one 24-hour period of time that commenced on Saturday, June 15, 2013.

While my husband taught the priesthood leaders of the area, I had the privilege of being with some of the sisters. I love our Russian sisters. They are spectacular!

That Saturday happened to be one of those rare spring planting days in Russia, so fewer than 100 of us were gathered.

When I stepped to the pulpit, I found myself saying something I'd never anticipated: "I'd like to get to know you by lineage. Please stand as the name of the tribe of Israel, as declared in your patriarchal blessing, is spoken.

"Gad?" A couple of women stood.

"Dan?" A couple more.

"Reuben?" A few more stood.

"Simeon?" More still.

"Naphtali?" More stood.

These women knew each other, but they didn't know each other's lineage.

As the names of the 12 tribes of Israel were announced—from Asher to Zebulon—and as the women stood, we were all amazed with what we were witnessing, feeling, and being taught.

We were being taught about the reality of the days in which we now live!

How many of the 12 tribes of Israel do you think were represented in that small gathering of fewer than 100 women—on that Saturday in Moscow?

Eleven! Eleven of the 12 tribes!

All but the tribe of Levi!

I went directly from that unforgettable gathering to the airport to meet my husband. We then flew to Yerevan, Armenia, where he was to create the first stake of Zion in that country the next day.

The first people we met as we got off plane in Armenia were the mission president and his wife.

The first thing she said to me, with a twinkle in her voice, was, "I've got Levi!"

Can you believe how fast the news of the 11 tribes had traveled from Moscow to Yerevan?

And further, just imagine our thrill when we met their missionaries the next day, one of whom—from Gilbert, Arizona, no less—was of the tribe of Levi!

When I was a little girl attending Primary in Raymond, Alberta, Canada, I was taught that in the last days before the Second Coming of the Savior, the 12 tribes would be gathered. That was always thrilling, and a little overwhelming, to think about.

So, imagine what it was like for me to *be with* children from *all* 12 tribes of Israel within one 24-hour period of time!

It was far beyond thrilling. And very overwhelming!

I couldn't believe it *then*. And I still can't get over it yet!

I know that many of us have heard stories of the 12 tribes gathering. The ones I heard were always far beyond secondhand stories. They went something like this: The sister-in-law of the cousin of the mailman of a stake patriarch told her aunt's father's brother-in-law's friend that the patriarch said the 12 tribes are gathering and that he had given patriarchal blessings to children from each tribe.

For some reason I never felt comfortable retelling those stories. (I wonder why?)

But within 24 hours commencing on June 15, 2013, I saw them *firsthand!* Children from all 12 tribes of Israel!

These are indeed the latter days!

There has *never* been a time like this in the history of this earth. Ever!

When I think of the extraordinary days in which we live, I think of two great young single adults, biological sisters, whom I met the day before my husband created in Moscow on June 5, 2011, the very first stake in Russia.

I asked them, "What does it mean to you that you are going to have a stake in Russia, right here in Moscow?"

They answered in unison and with a mix of surprise, awe, and enthusiasm in their voices: "This is serious!"

And the proof of how seriously they took the power, principles, and practices of the restored gospel of Jesus

Christ and His Church, *from that moment on,* is that two years later, each was serving a mission as a full-time representative of the Lord.

Indeed, this *is* serious. There has *never* been a more important time than right now to understand the gift our Father has given us as He allows us to make covenants with Him.

One young mother expressed our privilege so well. She said: "To be able to personally make a covenant with God makes me feel as though I matter. I really do have a purpose in the great plan of it all. There is no third party or agent 'signing' on my behalf or the Lord's. The promise, the covenant, I make is directly with the Lord!"

There has never been a more important time to understand the power to which we have access because of our covenants than right now! And when we understand the *gift* of our covenants—and the power of God that flows to us through them—we, like Nephi, will truly delight in the covenants of the Lord.[4]

The Power That Flows from Our Covenant of Sacrifice

I'll never forget a fascinating interchange I had with a young friend I'll call Amy. Amy and her husband are former institute students of mine. Each is bright, faithful,

There has never been a

more IMPORTANT TIME

to understand the

POWER

to which we have

ACCESS

because of

our covenants

than RIGHT NOW!

and always ready to learn and to serve. Late one Saturday evening, when my husband was out of town on assignment, I was working against the clock to complete a major project. An incoming email broke my concentration. The email was from Amy, and she was in distress.

She wrote: "I was asked to speak, last minute, at my ward Relief Society activity this Wednesday. The topic is stress. I sent out a survey last night to 75 of the women here in BYU married student housing to find out what is stressing them out. After receiving their responses, I realize that I NEED HELP!"

As I read through the survey responses that Amy forwarded to me, those young wives and mothers reported they were experiencing stress, depression, anxiety, and marital intimacy problems. They listed as the cause of their problems: school, finances, lack of sleep, housework, homework, feelings of failing at everything, and an inability to balance all of their responsibilities.

I wondered how I should respond to Amy. What would really make a difference for these women? And what could be offered, during a 22-minute Relief Society message, that could *possibly* reduce the real-life distress of these young mothers?

As I thought about Amy's difficult assignment, my experiences with family history and temple work filled my mind.

As counterintuitive as this may seem, I felt strongly impressed, in a way I could not deny, to encourage Amy to offer a 21-day experiment to her Relief Society sisters.

So, I emailed back: "Invite the sisters to make a sacrifice of time to the Lord by increasing their time in family history work and in temple work for the next 21 days."

Amy accepted this suggestion, and the results were remarkable!

Here are just three examples of what happened.

One young wife and mother wrote: "During the 21 days that I increased my temple attendance and my family history work, I not only felt happier, I felt a sense of relief. I felt a weight had been taken off my chest.

"When I made time to do these things—which is hard because we all are busy—I found that somehow I had more time to get other things done that needed to be done."

Another woman experienced a significant decrease in anxiety that had previously required medication. Her positive changes in mood, energy, and inspiration were so dramatic that she wrote: "My husband started to pray in gratitude for the increased presence of the Spirit in our home, which has occurred since I have been making sacrifices of time to the Lord in temple and family history work."

And yet another sister reported: "I have a two-year-old and just had a baby last week.

"The 21-day experiment helped with the end of my pregnancy.

"The sacrifice of time to do family history was something I could do sitting down, that was productive, and brought the Spirit!

"It gave me more purpose and helped me not to focus on the discomforts of the end of my pregnancy."

My suggestion to a group of overtaxed, exhausted young mothers might seem not only counterintuitive but almost cruel. And with results that seem highly improbable!

Why would I ask *any* woman, especially a young mother, who feels as though she's barely surviving, to make a sacrifice of time to the Lord?

But these young mothers proved that sacrifice works.

It works for women who have made covenants with God. Why?

Because when covenant women keep their covenants, they have greater access to the power of God!

The power of God flows into them, and that power, His power, generates—

- a decrease in stress
- an increase in energy

- more and clearer revelation for their lives
- renewed focus
- courage to make needed changes
- an increase in patience
- and more time for what matters!

That's what these young mothers taught me as they kept their covenant of sacrifice.

Elder D. Todd Christofferson taught that spiritual power comes to us as we make and keep our covenants:

"What is the source of . . . spiritual power, and how do we obtain it? The source is God. Our access to that power is through our covenants with Him."[5]

Further, Elder Christofferson was explicit in his counsel that "in times of distress, let your covenants be paramount, and let your obedience be exact."[6]

That's *exactly* what those young covenant women did!

They were in distress, they focused on their covenant of sacrifice—they let that covenant "be paramount"—and their "obedience [was] exact."

And what happened?

Their distress fell away.

An Invitation to Try an Experiment

Would you be willing to try an experiment?

What would happen if within the next six months,

you selected a 21-day period of time and then did *whatever* it took in order to make a sacrifice of time to the Lord by increasing the time you spend in doing family history and temple work during those 21 days?

What blessings, miracles, and other positive changes would come to your life?

Sacrifice does indeed bring forth the blessings of heaven,[7] because sacrifice is a law of heaven. And when we live according to *any* law of heaven, heaven responds. When we make a sacrifice to the Lord, a sacrifice that means something to Him, heaven is bound to respond.

Here's what Elder Dallin H. Oaks said about sacrifice:

"Just as the atoning sacrifice of Jesus Christ is at the center of the plan of salvation, we followers of Christ must make our own sacrifices to prepare for the destiny that plan provides for us."[8]

So, let's consider the following question:

Are you and I willing to give up something in our lives *right now* to the Lord, so that we can have breath-taking, ever-growing, ever-learning, even unbelievable, presently inconceivable experiences *forever?*[9]

Bishop Gérald Caussé stated: "The law of sacrifice requires the willingness to give up the things of the world—even the most precious things if necessary—for the sake of the gospel. We do it with unwavering faith

When we make a

sacrifice to the Lord,

a sacrifice

that MEANS SOMETHING

to Him, *heaven is*

BOUND TO RESPOND.

and confidence that these things will be returned to us a hundred fold in the eternities."[10]

Consider two examples that demonstrate the power that can flow into our lives *right now* when we keep our covenant of sacrifice.

Temple Worship and the Power of Sacrifice

A superb stake president and his wife, whom I'll call Michael and Linda, loved the temple and attended regularly. This stake president thought that if he told his stake members about the blessings and joy he and his wife felt when they attended, the stake members would be invigorated to attend the temple (which was just a short drive from his stake boundaries) much more frequently and regularly. However, nothing changed.

Michael was then inspired by a letter from the First Presidency inviting "temple-worthy members to consider ways in which more frequent daytime temple attendance could occur" and to "replace some leisure activities with temple service."[11]

While fasting and praying about these directives, Michael went to the temple and there had what almost seemed to him like a conversation[12] with the Lord. The words "they shall learn from their own experience" stayed in his mind.

His impression was that there needed to be a sacrifice

made if temple attendance in his stake were to increase, and in fact, each endowed member needed to be invited to make a sacrifice.

Michael talked with his counselors in the stake presidency about the sacred tutoring he had received in the temple. They talked about how to implement the teaching. All three members of the stake presidency then visited each ward in their stake and stood together at the pulpit to invite endowed members to be in the temple for one day—any day they chose—during the week before their stake conference and to do as many temple sessions in that day as would constitute a sacrifice for him or her.[13]

The results were remarkable. Temple attendance soared, not just during that particular week but throughout the year. Every measure of "real growth" in their stake increased.[14] Miracles happened. Those without temple recommends worked with their bishops to become worthy to attend the temple. They were ready to change their lives, to keep their covenants with the Lord with exactness. And to make and keep even more covenants! Children growing up in the stake heard these true accounts and wanted to be in the temple as soon as *they* could: at age 12 to do proxy baptisms for those now living on the other side of the veil.

The temple, the house of the Lord, became *the* organizing principle for the lives of the Saints in this stake.

And for years now this stake has continued the practice of inviting endowed members of the stake, twice a year, to make a special offering of one day of their time to the Lord in His temple. It is not unusual for stake members to complete over 2,000 endowments during *each* of those two weeks. Two thousand endowments a week for one stake is an inspiring statistic, but it is clearly just the tip of a thriving iceberg of steady spiritual growth and development which is the foundation of this stake of Zion.

Here is another example of the power of sacrifice.

Fast Offerings and the Power of Sacrifice

"[The] principle of sacrifice is fundamental to a true observance of the law of the fast."[15] A minimum fast offering is the value of the two meals not eaten while fasting. In 1977, however, President Spencer W. Kimball counseled the Latter-day Saints to pay very generous fast offerings:

"Sometimes we have been a bit penurious and figured that we had for breakfast one egg and that cost so many cents and then we give that to the Lord. I think that when we are affluent, as many of us are, that we ought to be very, very generous. . . .

"I think we should . . . give, instead of the amount we saved by our two meals of fasting, perhaps much, much more—ten times more where we are in a position to do it."[16]

President Kimball promised: "If we give a generous fast offering, we shall increase our own prosperity both spiritually and temporally."[17]

President Kimball's counsel and promise stayed in the heart and mind of one young father. Decades later, he was talking with his son and his son's friend about how to be wise with their finances and how to increase their financial stability.

The son told me about their experience:

"Dad told my friend William and me about President Kimball's counsel and promise and then said, 'If you want to secure your future, put President Kimball's promise to the test and make a generous fast offering.'

"That message really stuck with William, and the next month he and his wife increased their fast offering measurably. Over the course of the next few months, they were amazed, not that the Lord fulfilled His promise, but that the fulfillment was so clear and immediate. They received blessings in multiple aspects of their lives and in important ways they could never have imagined."[18]

William was so convinced about the blessings associated with paying a generous fast offering that as a member of his stake high council he began to share his experience with others throughout his stake. A number of individuals who heard him testify about the power of fasting and donating generously increased their own fast offerings and also saw an increase in blessings as a result.

Blessings come in many ways and at various times. But in whatever fashion and at whatever time, *the very best* blessings for us *always* come as we keep our covenants. Timing is the Lord's prerogative. President Henry B. Eyring counseled us that "we can create a barrier to knowing God's will or feeling His love for us: we can't insist on *our* timetable when the Lord has His own."[19]

There are all kinds of things we can sacrifice to the Lord.

Our will is the most important thing we can give Him.[20]

We know that how we use our time is important to Him.

Imagine what can happen as we make a sacrifice *of time* to the Lord by doing two things we know He really cares about: family history and temple work?

And why does the Lord care about family history and temple work? Because they bring His children Home.

During a 21-day period, make a sacrifice of time to the Lord by increasing your time spent in doing family history and temple work.

And then be prepared to be surprised. God is a great compensator.[21]

The Power That Flows from
Our Covenant of Service

Now, just as keeping our covenant of sacrifice will bring the power of God to our lives, so I've learned that the power of God also flows to us when we keep our *covenant of service.*

Although the world tells men to play nine holes of golf or to go on a vacation and tells women that the very best way to be rejuvenated is by going on a shopping spree or visiting a spa—I believe that *covenant* men and women are far more likely to be rejuvenated through serving, especially if they are able to delight in that covenant with others.

I learned that principle some years ago at BYU Women's Conference. I was serving then as the women's conference chair.

During our months of planning, several of us had the idea that adding a service component to the conference would be powerful.

The idea felt inspired. We thought others would cheer, but we were wrong.

Dead wrong.

Some on the committee felt strongly that a service project would backfire. One statement made during an energetic discussion is emblazoned upon my memory:

IMAGINE WHAT CAN HAPPEN

as we make a *sacrifice of time* to the

Lord by doing *two things*

we know He really cares about:

FAMILY HISTORY

⤳ *and* ⤝

TEMPLE WORK

"Women don't come to Women's Conference to serve. They come to relax and get away from it all!"

Gratefully, the Relief Society General Presidency saw wisdom in the idea, and ultimately the very first service event at a BYU Women's Conference unfolded.

That pioneering effort was thrilling!

It was successful beyond anything any of us imagined, even though the outcome pales in comparison to the service rendered at that conference now every year.

I am even more convinced now, years later, that weary covenant men and women are *revitalized* as the power of God flows into their lives when they keep their covenant of service. We were indeed *born to serve!* Our spirits remember our premortal covenant to serve, and they rejoice when we keep it.

One way we can keep our covenant to serve is by helping others prepare for, understand, and keep their covenants. Let me share two examples with you.

Example 1. Can you imagine a family home evening in which six children—the youngest aged three years—are lined up on chairs, *without* coloring books or quiet books, sitting very still for 20 minutes?

How long is 20 minutes?

"Almost the length of a Mr. Rogers episode," the children were told.

One courageous mother and father imagined it,

planned it, and pulled it off. And may I add that no heavy sedation for the parents or the children was involved!

The mother told me of their experience and what they did to prepare the children for the 20 minutes of focused, worshipful silence:

"My husband and I shared thoughts, read scriptures, and opened a discussion on what would be appropriate to think about during the reverent sacrament time. We talked about what we each might pray about during that quiet time, what our promises to our Father in Heaven have been and could be, and what we wanted to repent of that week. We talked about the importance of the special sacrament hymn. We bore witness of our Savior's love for us and of His Atonement. His Resurrection was proof of that love for us.

"We practiced acceptable behavior in our home in preparation for the time on Sunday when the sacrament would be blessed and passed to each of us. We talked about how we could have the Spirit more abundantly in our home during the week in preparation for *the most important time of our entire week:* partaking of the sacrament. And we learned that we could do it!"

Now that's "righteous, intentional parenting," a powerful term introduced by my husband in his April 2015 general conference address.[22]

Example 2. We know another couple who have been

devoted to righteous intentional parenting. I asked the husband to tell me of their efforts to teach their children about making promises as part of the process of their children's learning to make and keep covenants with God. He wrote the following to me:

"I will try to explain to you what I did as their father. When our children turned 16 years of age, I invited each one to meet with me for a special interview. After a prayer, I shared with each one the scripture contained in Doctrine and Covenants 138:47, which tells us that 'the Prophet Elijah was to plant in the hearts of the children the promises made to their fathers.'

"I shared my feelings about a father giving promises to his children and children doing the same for their father. I spoke of the promises I was giving to him or her, which included these promises: I will be always a good and faithful father to each one; I will be his or her best friend; I will help each one on all occasions; I will be always ready to give my life for him or her; I will try with all my heart to follow the example of our Lord Jesus Christ; I will honor the name of our family; I will keep the commandments; I will love and respect their mother and each of them, etc.

"After sharing with each child *my* promises I gave him or her one week to think, ponder, and pray about what we had talked about and then to return for another conversation in which he or she would give promises to me.

"They made a lot of beautiful promises, which included promises to keep the commandments, to keep the law of chastity *forever,* to be obedient, to be a good member of The Church of Jesus Christ of Latter-day Saints, to attend seminary and other Church meetings and activities, to be good students and honor our financial sacrifices to enable them to attend a good school, etc."

That is what one father did as part of his and his wife's efforts to help their children understand covenants.

And what happened?

Here is what this father wrote:

"I remember when our son was 17 years old. One evening we sat on the stairs of our home to talk. After a time I asked him about his relationship with girls. I asked if he respected them, if he was gentle and kind with them, etc. His answer was so powerful it touched my heart. He said, 'Daddy, do you remember that I promised you I would keep the law of chastity my entire life?'

"I gave him a very strong hug and with tears in my eyes, I told him I was proud of him. It was amazing to see that one conversation when he was 16 was lodged deep in his heart."

What a payday for that father! A father who had invested himself in serving his son by teaching him about promises, preparing him to make and keep covenants with God.

Angels above Us Are Doing More Than Silently Taking Notes

One of our hymns teaches us that "angels above us are silent notes taking" of each one of our actions.[23] I'm sure that is true. And when we keep our covenants, they are doing so much more.

The Prophet Joseph Smith declared that if we "live up to [our] *privilege,*" the angels will not be able to be restrained from being our associates.[24]

Our "privilege" includes our covenants.

Our covenants are a privilege.

Therefore, as we live up to our *covenants,* the angels will not be able to be restrained from being our associates.

We could also say it this way: As we keep our covenants, we can ask for angels to help us. Literally!

It was during Elder Jeffrey R. Holland's April 2010 general conference address that I first learned this truth. Elder Holland was giving counsel on how to guard against temptation. The one question I most needed to have answered at that time in my life, and which I took to that general conference, was *not* related to that subject,

As we live up to our *covenants,*

the angels

will not be able to be restrained

from being OUR ASSOCIATES.

but part of Elder Holland's prescription for success was *exactly* what I needed to hear.

He said, "Ask for angels to help you."[25]

He said it with such clarity, and yet he said it in a manner that implied this was something we all knew!

But for me it was an entirely new principle.

I wanted to call out, "Wait! Wait! What? You mean I could have been asking for angels to help me all this time?"

Without intending to sound too dramatic, I can say with all candor that Elder Holland's six words changed my life:

"Ask for angels to help you."

That counsel changed my prayers.

It changed my understanding of the very real help from heaven that is always available to us *as we keep our covenants.*

I started to ask for assistance from those on the other side of the veil from that moment on!

Now, I'm not talking about praying for fantasy angels with wings to magically fairy-dust our problems away.

I'm not talking about praying *to* angels.

I'm talking about praying to our Heavenly Father, in the name of Jesus Christ, for those on the other side to be "dispatched"[26] (Elder Holland's word) to assist us.

Perhaps a departed loved one could be sent to help you with whatever you need.

Can you imagine the effort it took those angels who pushed from the rear of handcarts as they helped the pioneers over the steep, snowy, windy, freezing, jagged terrain of Rocky Ridge?

If angels can manage *that*, they can certainly help you and me over our present-day Rocky Ridges!

One faithful covenant-keeping woman learned how real angels are and how ready they are to help when we are in despair. Her life had been turned upside down and her heart broken. She had recently learned that her husband had for many years chosen to betray her and break his covenants with God and with her. One night all alone with her thoughts, she sank into deep despair. She was without hope and could see no way to move ahead with her life. Darkness and dead ends were all she could see. Thoughts of ending her life seized hold of her mind.

After several hours of seriously contemplating her death, she suddenly felt prompted to walk to her basement. As she passed a bookshelf, her eyes were drawn to something she hadn't seen in decades, something that had been missing for years: her favorite photograph of herself as a young mother with her children. Seeing their trusting, loving faces looking up to her for guidance brought her to her senses. She knew in that instant that she could never take her life. She could never leave her children—who were now grown up with children of their own—in that manner. She marveled at how the Lord knew exactly the photograph that would help her *in an instant* to choose to live. She was amazed at the precise timing when the Lord sent His angels to find the framed, formerly lost photograph and place it *exactly where* she would see it. *Exactly when* she needed to see it.

We know the Lord gets His work done with the help of His angels! And who are His angels?

President Joseph F. Smith declared: "When messengers are sent to minister to the inhabitants of this earth, they are not strangers, but from the ranks of our kindred [and] friends. . . . In like manner, our fathers and mothers, brothers, sisters and friends who have passed away from this earth, having been faithful, and worthy to enjoy these rights and privileges, may have a mission given them to visit their relatives and friends upon the earth again, bringing from the divine Presence messages of love, of warning, of reproof and instruction to those whom they had learned to love in the flesh."[27]

So, could you use a little more help in your life?

If so, keep your covenants with more exactness than you ever have before!

And then ask for angels (a.k.a. your ancestors and other loved ones) to help you with *whatever* you need.

Or ask for them to be dispatched to help those you love!

One bishop, who understood the angel resources available to him, said to his wife at the end of a long, extremely grueling day, "I have done everything I can for the members of our ward. Now all I can do is ask for angels to be assigned to help the rest!"

So, does your child need help?

Is your husband in trouble?

Does your wife need more support?

Does your aunt need comfort?

Does your best friend need direction?

If so, ask for angels to be assigned to help them!

As a covenant-keeping man or woman, you can do that!

One of my former institute students, whom I'll call Barbara, followed through with that suggestion with thrilling results.

Barbara has served as proxy for many of my ancestors.

During a few temple sessions, Barbara had special experiences with a woman named Genevieve and with Genevieve's biological sisters. Barbara felt a deep connection with them.

So, she prayed and asked if Genevieve and her sisters, all of whom now live on the other side of the veil, could be dispatched to help Barbara's own sister, who lives on *this* side of the veil.

Barbara's sister had not been active in the Church for

years, and she was having heart-wrenching difficulties with some rigorous life events.

Here are Barbara's words:

"I prayed that my sister could find peace in this world, that she could find direction back to Heavenly Father, and that the sisters of Genevieve could help her find her way back and watch over her in this process.

"A few weeks later my sister told me that she was taking her three boys to Church! Later she asked me how to get her patriarchal blessing. The eldest boy turned eight this summer and was baptized. And my sister is now attending temple preparation classes."

How can we explain such miracles?

Moroni tells us: "My beloved brethren [and sisters], have miracles ceased? Behold I say unto you, Nay; neither have angels ceased to minister unto the children of men. . . . And the office of their ministry is to call men [and women] unto repentance, and to fulfil and to do the work of the covenants of the Father."[28]

COVENANTS AND THE POWER OF PERSPECTIVE

Now let's consider the power of perspective that our covenants can provide.

We know that our covenants with God did not start here on this earth, and they will not end here.

We know that we made covenants with God premortally.[29]

Perhaps that's one of the reasons we "shouted for joy"![30] We are grateful for the veil of forgetfulness. It heightens the testing feature of our mortal probation.

And wow! What a test this is turning out to be—for each one of us!

But if the veil were lifted and we could look back, we would see ourselves as His spirit sons and daughters making premortal covenants with God, our Heavenly Father.

Elder Neal A. Maxwell taught that we made premortal covenants about particular assignments, callings, and missions we would fulfill here on earth.[31] Perhaps that's why some callings bring such a reassuring feeling—at the very same time we feel so ill-prepared!

Fulfilling the wonderful missions for which we were sent to earth is one of the sure ways we can find peace and joy as we journey through this "spook alley"[32] of mortal life.

We made covenants regarding those with whom we associated premortally. One woman had the following experience when she and some friends dedicated an entire

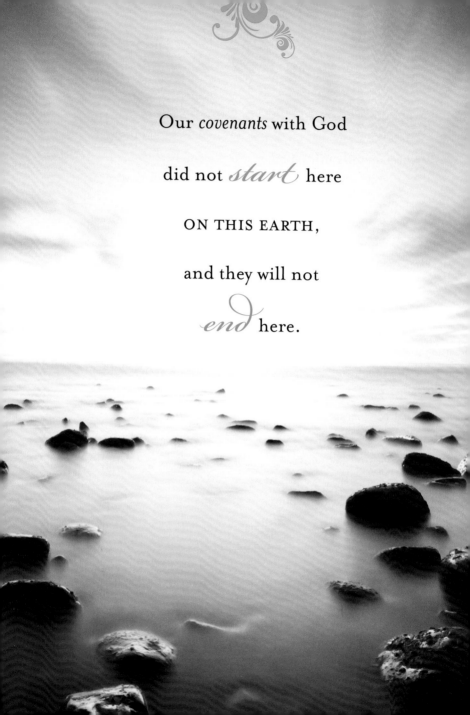

Our *covenants* with God

did not *start* here

ON THIS EARTH,

and they will not

end here.

day to serving in the temple. The temple president noticed them and initiated a conversation. Here is what my friend reported:

"The temple president talked to us about the passage in the Doctrine and Covenants where it says that Elijah will plant in the hearts of the children the promises made to their fathers.[33] He talked about how some of those promises may have been *us* promising loved ones that we would help them get their temple work completed. He also said that he wondered if finding out when we were coming to earth was something like receiving a mission call."

He then said, "Imagine that you were told, 'You are going to be in South Jordan, Utah, in 2014, and there will be 141 temples on the earth at that time.' Perhaps while you were preparing to come to earth, spirits who would live on earth at a time when they would be *unable* to receive their ordinances came up to you and said, 'You are going down to earth when there will be 141 temples on the earth. When you are there, will you please not forget me?' And you said, 'I promise I will not forget you!'"

Elder John A. Widtsoe taught that we covenanted premortally to be partners with the Father and the Son in Their work to "bring to pass the immortality and eternal life of man"![34]

Elder Widtsoe said: "In our preexistent state, in the

day of the great council, we made a certain agreement with the Almighty. The Lord proposed a plan. We accepted it. Since the plan is intended for *all* men, we became parties to the salvation of *every* person under that plan. We agreed, right then and there, to be not only saviors for ourselves but measurably, saviors for the whole human family. We went into a partnership with the Lord. The working out of the plan became then not merely the Father's work, and the Savior's work, but also our work. The least of us, the humblest, is in partnership with the Almighty in achieving the purpose of the eternal plan of salvation."[35]

What an amazing covenant! To be partners with the Father and the Son to help save the *entire* human family?![36] When we made that spectacular premortal covenant, did we ever imagine just how much time we would need to spend shepherding and rescuing others or how many hours studying and teaching and preaching the gospel?

Did we have *any clue* about the number of hours we would need to spend on the FamilySearch website? And the numerous hours in the temple that we would need to devote so that we could fulfill *just that one* stunning premortal covenant?

Did we have any idea about how many activities we would need to *give up doing* so we would have time to help others return Home—to receive all that the Father hath?[37]

What other covenants did we make premortally? And what effect can they have on our lives right now?

After the professional experiences I had for 25 years as a professor of marriage and family therapy and the life experiences I've had in the decade since then, I strongly believe that if we could see ourselves making our premortal covenants with our Heavenly Father, *any and all* of our anguish, grief, and heartache would fall away. And we would say, "Oh, now I remember! This heart-wrenching situation makes sense now!"[38]

That's the power of the premortal perspective our covenants can provide!

The Power of the Connection Perspective

Now, consider this truth:

Commencing with Adam and Eve, *all* righteous men and women who love the Lord and have accepted His gospel have made covenants with Him!

Think of *any* of the covenant women and men down through the ages whom we love and admire—from Sarah and Rebekah to Sariah and Rachel; from Abraham and Isaac to Lehi and Jacob; from Noah and his wife to Daniel and his; from Peter and his wife to James and John and theirs; from Adam and Eve to Joseph Smith and Emma and Eliza.

Each of these men and women made *the very*

same covenants with God that you and I have made![39] Therefore, our covenants with God connect us with other men and women who have made covenants with God.

I love to think of that!

The very fact that temple covenants and ordinances seem *so different* from experiences during our Sunday worship meetings is yet another testimony of their truthfulness. They are ancient!

The "ancient of days"—meaning Adam, with Eve—received those covenants, our very covenants, from God![40] How thrilling is that?

Now, just for a moment, imagine two gigantic mirrors placed with their reflecting surfaces facing each other.

Picture you and me with a chapel full of faithful—not perfect but faithful—Latter-day Saint men and women who are striving to keep their covenants[41] standing in front of one of the mirrors and looking into it with the other mirror parallel behind us.

What would we see?

We would see numberless images of men and women stretching into infinity.

Can you picture that in your mind's eye?

Freeze-frame that image.

As you look at that image, you are seeing the number of covenant men and women with whom you and I are connected *each and every time* we make a covenant with God!

And each and every time we keep those sacred obligations!

Brothers, if you were to picture yourself standing with your priesthood quorum looking into those double mirrors each and every time you were surfing the web, would it make it easier to stand for truth and righteousness as a worthy priesthood holder as you chose which sites to visit while you maneuver through entreating and entrapping pop-ups as you search for information to assist you with your employment? How would that image of those millions of other covenant-keeping men help you with your Internet selections?

My husband, speaking to the brethren, strongly counseled: "Your highest priesthood duty is to care for your wife. That is your eternal charge."[42]

Do you realize that one of the most important ways you can "care for your wife" is to be impeccably true and faithful to her as you spend time on the Internet?

One husband, understanding the strength that can come from joining with other covenant keepers, said: "The fact that I have made covenants with God, and some also with my wife, helps give me strength when life's challenges come. These covenants remind me that I am part of something much greater than just myself, and I can lean on others who have made covenants for their help and support because we share a deep, mutually binding interest."

Now, sisters, let's talk about our time with social media.

It has been said that the present fascination some women have with social media is the need women have to feel connected with other women!

To support each other, to know what's happening in each other's lives, to have other women know and approve of what we're doing.

We want witnesses for our lives!

So, sisters, if you saw yourself looking into the double mirrors with the faithful covenant-keeping women in your life whom you love and admire, let's consider this question:

Do we, as covenant women, need more friends on Facebook, or do we need to experience more of the beautifully familiar, unmistakably divine feelings of being connected with—perhaps more accurately, reconnected with—*millions* of other women who have made covenants with God?

On a day when we don't think *anyone* cares about us and our struggles or all we've been trying to do, what would happen if we took just a moment to look, with our mind's eye, into those double mirrors and see the truth?

Because the truth is that *each and every day* you and I *let* our covenants influence our thoughts and words and actions, we are inseparably connected to millions and millions of covenant women. Women from the beginning of time down through each and every gospel dispensation!

Now, those are friends we hope will "like" us!

The Power of the Perspective of Those on the Other Side of the Veil

And now, to talk about another perspective, let me tell you of an unexpected journey I've been on for the past two and a half years.

To do so, let's start with some questions:

Could you use more help in your life?

Do you feel lonely or disconnected from others?

Are you unsettled about your life?

Do you have a yearning to be involved in something really meaningful?

Do you question if you're making a real difference *anywhere?*

Are you weary of wrestling with an old temptation?

One key to dealing with concerns such as these, as well as many others that wrench our heartstrings, is (drum roll, please . . .) family history work.

When you hear the words *family history,* do you

When we let our covenants influence

our THOUGHTS *and* WORDS *and* ACTIONS,

we are *inseparably connected*

to *millions* of covenant women and men—

from the beginning of time down

through every gospel dispensation!

go into a coma? Believe me, until recently I could have matched my coma with yours any day. It used to be that if I wanted to have a really good sleep, all I needed to do was to *think* about doing family history work. Just the *prospect* of doing it was better than ether!

Something changed for me when I listened to, read, and studied repeatedly Elder Richard G. Scott's general conference talk of October 2012, entitled "The Joy of Redeeming the Dead." Even though I had traveled in my twenties to Switzerland and Scotland to visit places my ancestors had lived, had been locked in a graveyard, and had lugged with me from one city, even one country, to another the many boxes filled with family history which my grandmother bequeathed me in my late teens; even though I had attended and even taught the family history/genealogy course in my various wards over the years; and even though I had a membership in Family Search—I had never actually gone online to find qualifying dates and places. I had never filled out a Family Ordinance Request form (F.O.R.)—I didn't even know what that was! I had never taken an F.O.R. to the temple to have the ordinance cards printed out—I didn't know where to go inside the temple to have that done. And even though I loved attending the temple and did so regularly, I had never served as proxy for even *one* of *my* ancestors. Never.

Elder Scott's talk changed all of that. When he spoke,

it felt as though he was speaking directly to me and allowing over 15 million others to listen in.

At the end of his talk when he said, "What about you? Have you prayed about your ancestors' work?"[43] I heard it as, "What about you, Wendy? Have you prayed about *your* ancestors' work?"

No, I hadn't. And I hadn't even thought about doing so. The thing I had done *the very most* about my ancestors was to feel guilty. And I had done a lot of that!

When Elder Scott said, "This work is a spiritual work,"[44] I believed him. And I started to think about what I needed to do to make family history work a spiritual work for me.

I was led to do several things, including (1) work in silence, which was not natural for someone who loves music as much as I do, and (2) create a spiritual environment in a little room—formally a storage room—which we have now dedicated to family history. One day in the temple I had an impression that this little family history room needed to be one of the most sacred rooms in our home. My experience with a stake patriarch came to my mind. When I asked how he prepared to give a patriarchal blessing, I anticipated him saying something like, "Oh, I study the attributes and blessings of the 12 tribes of Israel. I read my scriptures. I pray. I go to the temple."

Instead, he said, "I begin by vacuuming."

At that point, our family history room needed far more than a good vacuuming! And yet, I could feel that I was not supposed to spend a lot of time "organizing" my family history boxes and files in order to create a clean, uncluttered environment. I had taken that approach before—for decades—over and over again. A multitude of anguishing hours spent sorting and filing always resulted in *only* a small dent in what my grandmother had given to me—and yet, *not one* new ancestor, even with the investment of all of those hours and all of that energy, had been given the privilege of making covenants with God and receiving essential ordinances!

Elder Scott's message urged me to *do something different* this time. So, without going into details, let me just say that inexpensive, ready-made white curtains hide a multitude of boxes!

As I worked in this light-filled environment, I found myself praying, "Please lead me to those who are ready to make covenants with Thee and receive their ordinances." That prayer opened the heavens for me. That environment and that prayer helped me to *feel* which branches, limbs, and sometimes twigs of my family tree to pursue.

I remember one night teetering out on a twig and wondering what I was doing way out there. Then suddenly a woman on that twig married a man on a twig from two nights before! I can still feel the thrill of noting their marriage date and place so they could be sealed as husband and wife! This work is indeed a spiritual work!

When Elder Scott asked, "Can you see that you don't have to be [a genealogist] anymore?"[45] I believed him. And that truth has helped me more than once when I have been doing research. When I hit a tough spot and find myself wishing I had more genealogical skills, I remind myself, "Wendy, you don't have to be a genealogist."

Because of the prayer I offer to commence each research session ("Please lead me to those who are ready to make covenants with Thee and receive their ordinances"), whenever I hit a block in finding information that would qualify a person for his or her ordinances, I think about the possibilities behind the block: Could it be that this person is just now "taking the discussions" from missionaries on the other side of the veil? Has this person not yet received and embraced the gospel of Jesus Christ?

If that feels like the reason for the block, I move on to someone else who *is* ready and eager to make covenants and receive his or her ordinances. I will go back to the gospel investigator later.

When Elder Scott said, "Do you . . . want a sure way to eliminate the influence of the adversary in your life?"[46] I absolutely did. And I determined right then to do as much family history work as I possibly could in order to keep the destructive deceptions of the adversary out of our home.

When Elder Scott taught that some sacrifice would be involved, I believed him. But what could I possibly sacrifice? And then he counseled, "Set aside those things in your life that don't really matter. Decide to do something that will have eternal consequences."[47]

I wanted to do just that, but I couldn't imagine what I could set aside. I thought I was using my time *really* well on things that *really* mattered. I was certainly exhausted enough! Wasn't that an indication?

Then I remembered the time I spent by myself playing Scrabble on my iPad. I didn't think that little bit of time could make any difference, but I set Scrabble aside for two months. Now, that may not seem like much of a sacrifice, but for me, I was giving up a bit of harmless fun.[48]

When Elder Scott taught that family history is "a monumental effort of cooperation on both sides of the veil, where help is given in both directions,"[49] I believed him, and I have found it to be absolutely true. Over and over again, I have been amazed to "coincidentally" meet a person who could help me or out of the blue to find a piece of information I needed. There is no doubt in my mind that angels *from both sides of the veil*[50] are assigned to help us with this work. We'll *never* be alone in our efforts to do family history work. Never.

So, what do we need so we can do *our part* in family history work? What has been holding us back? What is it we don't understand? All we have to do is ask our Heavenly Father in the name of Jesus Christ for what we need. Ask. Ask. Ask. And then follow each and every prompting.

Undoubtedly, family history work is the Lord's work. And, we know He can do His own work.[51] Therefore, think of how generous He is to let us be involved!

By the way, we now have zero excuses for failing to be involved. Why? Because the Lord has now provided us with "the doctrine, the temples, and the technology" to succeed.[52]

I have experienced for myself that the Lord will provide *everything* we need to be successful in doing family history work and with the temple work related to it, including the inspiration, the information, the energy, the answers, the proxies, and even the time and the desire. All we have to do is ask and show that we are serious in wanting to help.

THREE TRUTHS THAT CHANGED MY LIFE

Within the first two weeks of trying this new approach to family history, I learned three things I can never forget:

1. Those on the other side are very much alive—and perhaps not all that cheerful about being called "dead."

2. Those on the other side are eager—no, actually they are desperate—to receive their saving and exalting ordinances. And they know when and where their ordinances will be done for them. Let me tell you of an experience we had.

It has become part of my husband's morning routine to ask me if I have any ordinance cards or any Family Ordinance Request forms that he can drop off at the temple before going to his office. One morning he left with ordinance cards we had prepared for 76 people who were ready to make covenants with God and be baptized. One of those people was Annie McIntyre.

When my husband returned to the temple later in the day to pick up the cards, after the young men and women had completed the proxy baptisms and confirmations, he was told that a remarkable experience had occurred in the baptistry that day. As the young woman who was to be baptized for Annie McIntyre looked at Annie's name, she remembered the dream she had had the night before. In her dream was a woman named Annie McIntyre. The young woman had never heard that name before and didn't give it a second thought after waking up. But in the baptismal font when she saw and heard Annie's name, the young woman burst out,

"I know this woman! She came to me in my dream last night and said that I would be baptized for her today!" Yes, indeed, our young women will dream dreams and see visions.[53]

After completing Annie's proxy baptism, the young woman was confirmed for several women, including Annie. During the proxy confirmation of Annie, the young woman experienced an overwhelming rush of emotion as she heard Annie McIntyre's name again. She knew that feeling was a confirmation that Annie was grateful her work had been done. Annie McIntyre had, by proxy, made her baptismal covenant with God that day. She had been baptized and confirmed a member of the Lord's Church. Annie's prison gates had been unlocked.

Covenants, and *only* covenants with their associated ordinances, have the power to unlock the gates behind which our ancestors live. So, as wonderful as it is to know stories about Grandma (or Annie)—for example, that she loved peaches and poems—if we don't do *whatever it takes* to ensure that she has the privilege to make covenants with God and receive her essential ordinances—guess what? Grandma (or Annie) is still in prison!

And I'm not sure just how long she's going to be cheerful about that!

3. The third thing I learned is that we are *the* only church on the planet with the power and authority from

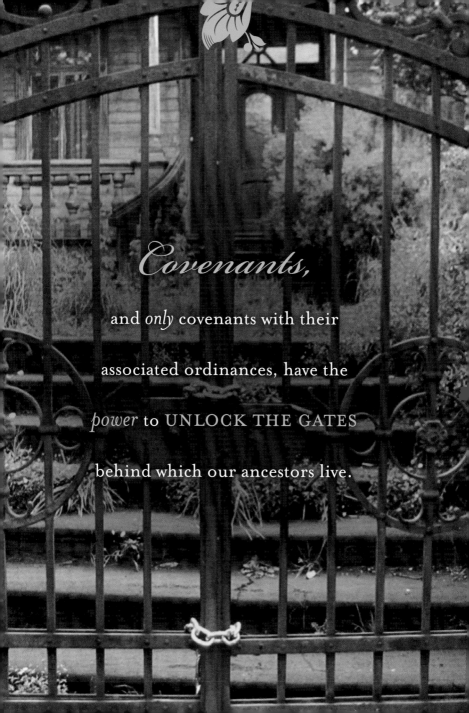

Covenants,

and *only* covenants with their

associated ordinances, have the

power to UNLOCK THE GATES

behind which our ancestors live.

God to perform these essential ordinances. We cannot share, divide up, or delegate any part of this work to any other church. No other church has the priesthood keys, authority, and power of Jesus Christ to perform these proxy ordinances. It is as simple and profoundly true as that.

Anguish and Urgency

Those three truths brought forth a growing anguish and urgency within me: an intense anguish about those on the other side who, without redeeming covenants[54] and essential ordinances, are unable to progress, accompanied by a relentless urgency to help.

Each time I opened my computer and began doing family history research on the FamilySearch website and on Ancestry.com, I found that my mind was filled with words attributed to Oskar Schindler—even though it had been over 30 years since I had studied Schindler's life.

Let me give you a little background on Schindler.

There are countless examples of men and women who have lived through circumstances that have caused them to reassess what really matters. One such man was Oskar Schindler.

By outwitting Hitler and the Nazis, Schindler is credited with saving more Jews from the gas chambers than any other person.

Schindler was a German industrialist and a member of the Nazi party. He was an opportunist who was initially motivated only by making money, lots of money.

Because of his experiences during the course of World War II, however, Schindler's passion for making money shifted to a passion for saving lives. People's lives began to matter to him, and he commenced to use his extraordinary initiative, his tenacity, and his dedication to save the lives of his Jewish employees who worked for him in his factories. In order to keep his Jewish workers safe from the gas chambers, where they would have been killed, Schindler was required to give larger and larger bribes and gifts of luxury items to the Nazi officials. Schindler literally purchased the lives of over a thousand Jews.[55]

There have been many accounts made of his life—movies made, books written. One portrayal of his life includes a conversation with his wife. This took place when Schindler's focus was on making money. He was just starting out with a new business venture in Poland. As I recall, the conversation went something like this:

Wife: "They won't soon forget the name Schindler here."

Schindler: "Everybody remembers him.

"'He did something extraordinary!'

"'He did something no one else did.'

"'He came here with nothing—a suitcase—and built a bankrupt company into a major manufacturing company and left with a steamer trunk—two steamer trunks—filled with money. All the riches of the world!'"

Now compare that conversation filled with hubris and arrogance to a conversation he had with his trusted Jewish accountant several years later. At this point, Schindler was filled with humility and regret. Again as I recall, the conversation went something like this:

Schindler: "I could have got more people.

"I could have got more! If I had more money.

"I threw away so much money.

"You have no idea. If I just had more money.

"I didn't do enough.

"This car. Why did I keep this car? Ten people right there. Ten people. Ten more people.

"This pin. Two more people.

"This is gold! Two more people. It would have given me two more people. It would have given me one more person.

"One more person.

"One more person.

"I could have gotten one more person. And I didn't."

We all know the feeling of anguish and regret.

We know the feeling of urgency.

We know that compelling feeling of wanting to do more. Much more.

Schindler's anguished words about why he wasted so much money, his desperate wish that he had saved more people—*even one more person*—kept coming to my mind. His words haunted me.

My longing to do more, to find more people, to use my time more wisely, led me to hear Schindler's words in my mind this way:

"I could have found more people!

"I could have found more! If I had more time.

"I wasted so much time.

"You have no idea. If I just had more time.

"I didn't do enough.

"That dinner I went to. Why did I go to that dinner? By the time I got ready, drove to the event, which wasn't that important, made small talk with people, and drove back home . . .

"Ten people right there. Ten people. Ten more people.

"Shopping for that scarf—which I didn't find—two people.

"Two—more—people!

"That wasted time shopping would have given me two more people.

"I could have found two more people.

"I could have found ONE more person.

"ONE more person.

"One more person.

"I could have found one more person.

"And—I didn't!"

Now, please don't misunderstand. I am *not* saying that shopping is bad or that going to dinners is bad or that filling any number of other kinds of obligations is regrettable or wasteful. We all have responsibilities and needs—and one of those needs is to spend time with others: to serve them, mentor them, create uplifting memories with them, and love them. We all have the challenge of achieving some kind of reasonable balance in our lives, whatever that means.

A Sign That It's Time

As my husband and I travel, we see many signs. There is one in every airport that chokes me up every time: *Passengers only beyond this point.* I immediately think of those on the other side of the veil who are locked in prison, unable to move forward with their lives, to learn, to grow, to be with their families. The *only* way they can become "passengers" is by our efforts here on earth to find their qualifying information and perform their proxy ordinances. We hold the key to their release.[56]

Brigham Young boldly spoke the following on January 1, 1877, at the dedication of the St. George Temple. He died less than eight months later. Read his message with that important context in mind. These are literally some of his famous last words:

"What do you suppose the fathers would say if they could speak from the dead? Would they not say, 'We have lain here thousands of years, here in this prison house, waiting for this dispensation to come? Here we are, bound and fettered, in the association of those who are filthy?' What would they whisper in our ears? Why, if they had the power the very thunders of heaven would be in our ears, if we could but realize the importance of the work we are engaged in. All the angels in heaven are looking at this little handful of people, and stimulating them to the salvation of the human family. So also are the devils in hell looking at this people, too, and trying to overthrow us, and the people are still shaking hands with the servants of the devil, instead of sanctifying themselves and calling upon the Lord and doing the work which he has commanded us and put into our hands to do. When I think upon this subject, I want the tongues of seven thunders to *wake up the people*."[57]

Now, if Brigham Young can't wake us up to the urgency to be involved in family history *like we never have before*, I can guarantee you that our ancestors can! Just ask my husband. If he is looking for me in the middle of the night, he knows where to find me: our little family history room.

Remember those three things I learned in the first two weeks of my new approach to family history work? I also learned one more thing: Family history is really fun! Even more fun than Scrabble!

Because of experiences I've had while doing family history research, I am now a woman *desperately driven* by the desire not to waste time that I could spend helping those who are *desperate for covenants*. And no one is more surprised than I am. Now, for me, supersleuthing a mother's maiden name trumps watching any detective movie I used to enjoy! (This is not to say that I don't enjoy a good movie from time to time, though.)

So, if you'd like a little more joy in your life,

• a little more meaning,

• more heart-to-heart connections,

• more focus, energy, motivation,

• more of so many wonderful things,

make time to help those on the other side *make covenants* with God!

As you do so, the power of God will flow into your life in an unprecedented way.

What else can we do to keep and increase the flow of God's power in our lives? President Gordon B. Hinckley taught a great truth following the dedication of the Conference Center in October 2000. In the concluding session of that general conference, President Hinckley's parting words included this counsel:

"The great 'Hosanna' salutation in which we participated this morning should remain an unforgettable experience. From time to time, we can repeat quietly in our minds, when we are alone, those beautiful words of worship."[58]

If it is good for us to repeat quietly in our minds, when we are alone, the beautiful words of worship of the Hosanna salutation, wouldn't it be good for us to follow that same pattern with other beautiful words of worship?

What about the beautiful words of our baptismal and temple covenants and other sublime words spoken in the temple?

There is spiritual power in the words of our covenants.

Do we know the words?

Do we know what we said we would do?

Do we know what the Lord has promised?

Sometimes when we hear words frequently, they can

There is

spiritual power

in the words of

our *covenants.*

DO WE KNOW THE WORDS?

become background noise rather than a foreground focus to help us worship.

But we can change that!

We can make a personal plan for learning and remembering the words of our covenants.

It will take some effort. But we can do it!

The Power of the Covenants We Make Each Time We Partake of the Sacrament

How would our experience with the sacrament change if we imagined the Savior to be the one blessing the bread and water—just as He did for His Twelve Apostles?

And then, if the Savior stood before us and, while offering the emblems to us and looking directly into your eyes and mine, said:

"Are you willing to take upon you MY name this week?

"Are you willing to always remember ME?

"Are you willing to keep MY commandments this week?"

And what would change for us as we witnessed our willingness by eating the bread and drinking the water—and concurrently heard in our minds and felt in our hearts these words as we covenanted with our Heavenly Father:

"I now covenant with Thee that I am willing to take upon me the name of Thy Son this week.

"I now covenant with Thee that I am willing to always remember Him.

"I now covenant with Thee that I am willing to keep His commandments this week."

Perhaps we would feel even more of the power of our covenants with God if, at the end of each of those three sacred sentences, we added something specific to what is happening in our lives, such as, "as I work on that huge and really overwhelming project this week" or "as I seek to eat more healthfully" or "as I seek to forgive."

In this manner, the words that would fill our minds as the sacrament is passed might be these: "I now covenant with Thee, Heavenly Father, that I am willing to always remember Thy Son as I work on that huge and really overwhelming project this week."

Would we then truly experience a cleansing of our spirits[59] and "the wounds of [our] spirit[s] being healed, and [our] load[s] . . . lifted?"[60]

The Power of the Covenants
We Make in the Temple

And what about our temple covenants?

What can change for us as we learn, feel deeply, and remember the words of our temple covenants?

One of my former institute students (I'll call her Jean) had the following experience: Jean was put on bed rest during her second pregnancy and couldn't attend the temple for a little while.

She wrote: "I was sincerely struggling with feelings of being pulled so many different ways and of entering a new season of life that just didn't lend itself to weekly temple attendance at that point.

"It was in response to these feelings and prayerful pleadings that the words entered my mind, 'You may not always be able to go through the temple, but you are always able to have the temple go through you.'

"That was my answer and the one I so desperately needed!"

Jean continued: "Now I daily repeat the words we say in the temple (in my mind, of course) every morning as I get ready for the day.

"I reverently and with power say those words in my mind.

"I recovenant and rededicate myself each new day."

Now, clearly, Jean had been paying close attention during her previous weekly time in the temple.

For many of us, we can start now.

Each time we go to the temple, we can really focus on and learn the words of one more covenant or perhaps those of one more associated ordinance.

And then we can do what President Hinckley advised: "From time to time, we can repeat quietly in our minds, when we are alone, those beautiful words of worship."

A dear friend recently did just that on a day when she didn't feel well and yet was less than an hour away from needing to fulfill a major and highly stressful assignment. It seemed impossible!

She wrote: "As I waited alone in my car before the event and because I physically didn't feel well, I chose to focus on the words of the initiatory ordinance.

"As those words went through my mind, I actually started to feel a little bit better. Plus, they gave me a feeling of peace and assurance that somehow I'd get through the assignment." And she did.

Just think of the healing power and the enabling power that is available to us through sacred words of worship!

COVENANT KEEPERS

My husband taught this profound truth: "The greatest compliment that can be earned here in this life is to be known as a covenant keeper."[61]

As we are covenant keepers, our covenants change everything in our lives—for the better!

They change our identity and ultimate destination.

They change the road we're traveling on through this life, because now we're on the covenant path that leads back Home![62]

And no worldly GPS can ever find that road!

As covenant keepers, what we want out of life; what we are willing to spend our time, energy, and money on; what we think is entertaining; what we think is appealing—all change.

How we feel about others, how connected we feel *to* others, how we care about, and care for, others—all change.

As covenant keepers, we eagerly bring our very best to each calling we have, to every opportunity to serve. Our desire to be someone the Lord can count on increases exponentially. *No matter what* He asks us to do!

As covenant keepers, we find that how we feel about fasting and fast offerings, about tithing and about the temple, about obedience and sacrifice, about attending our meetings on Sunday, and about the Sabbath day[63] itself—changes.

As covenant keepers, we find that how we feel about the Savior changes forever!

He is real to us in a way He's never been before.

How we feel about His Atonement—changes.

We relish repentance.[64]

And we seek gifts of the Spirit, one by one, to turn our weak things into strengths![65]

As covenant keepers, we find that our prayers change—because we are now bound to Heavenly Father, and we're tied closer than ever before to our Savior Jesus Christ![66]

Personal revelation becomes something we prepare for and expect![67]

As covenant keepers, we find that our past, present, and future can all change!

Everything can change for the better—as we keep our covenants.

Including our very nature![68]

So, in the words of Elder Jeffrey R. Holland: "If you have made covenants, keep them.

"If you haven't made them, make them.

"If you have made them and broken them, repent and repair them."[69]

These latter days are OUR DAYS!

Are we ready?

We can be—as we make and keep our covenants with God.

We can be *morally strong* covenant-keeping men and

MAKING COVENANTS

with God calls forth the *divine* within us.

Keeping our covenants with God

ALLOWS HIM

to pour His *divine power* into us.

women who are sin-resistant Saints.[70] Men and women who, because of time spent in the temple, know how to deal with the adversary and how to pray with power!

We can be *diligent* covenant-keeping women and men who are true disciples of Jesus Christ in this digital age and who know how to use technology—righteously![71]

We can be *wise* covenant-keeping men and women who eagerly remove from our lives *anything* that is preventing us from *receiving even more* of God's power.

We can be *articulate* covenant-keeping women and men who are consistently seeking to understand the doctrine of Jesus Christ, so that we are not swayed by every "wind of doctrine"[72] that blows through a blog!

We can be *enlightened* covenant-keeping men and women who seek to understand more about our covenants. Women and men who know that when we let the Lord know we are serious about learning more, *He* will teach us!

It is my testimony that there is *nothing* more important than making covenants with God and then keeping them with increasing precision. Making covenants with God calls forth the divine within us. And keeping our covenants with God allows Him to pour His divine power into us.

NOTES

1. President David O. McKay said: "I believe there are few, even temple workers, who comprehend the full meaning and power of the temple endowment. Seen for what it is, it is the step-by-step ascent into the Eternal Presence" (quoted in Truman G. Madsen, *The Highest in Us* [1978], 103).

   President Marion G. Romney said: "When Jacob traveled from Beersheba toward Haran, he had a dream in which he saw himself on the earth at the foot of a ladder that reached to heaven where the Lord stood above it. He beheld angels ascending and descending thereon, and Jacob realized that the covenants he made with the Lord there were the rungs on the ladder that he himself would have to climb in order to obtain the promised blessings—blessings that would entitle him to enter heaven and associate with the Lord.

   "Because he had met the Lord and entered into covenants with him there, Jacob considered the site so sacred that he named the place Bethel, a contraction of Beth-Elohim, which means literally 'the House of the Lord'" ("Temples—The Gates to Heaven," *Ensign,* Mar. 1971, 16).

2. "There is no gift greater than the gift of salvation" (D&C 6:13).

3. Holland, "Keeping Covenants: A Message for Those Who Will Serve a Mission," *Liahona,* Jan. 2012, 49.

4. "My soul delighteth in the covenants of the Lord" (2 Nephi 11:5).

5. Christofferson, "The Power of Covenants," *Ensign,* May 2009, 20.

6. Ibid., 22.

7. "Praise to the Man," *Hymns of The Church of Jesus Christ of Latter-day Saints* (1985), no. 27.

8. Oaks, "Sacrifice," *Ensign,* May 2012, 22.

9. See Tad R. Callister, *The Infinite Atonement* (2000), 220–49.

10. Quoted in R. Scott Lloyd, "Bishop Caussé: Help Missionaries Elevate Personal Consecration," *Church News,* July 9, 2014, lds.org.

11. "Letter from the First Presidency," *Ensign,* Mar. 2004, 45.

12. D&C 124:39—"in your most holy places wherein you *receive* conversations" (emphasis added).

13. Linda and Michael determined to participate in five endowment sessions for each of five days in the designated week. That would be their offering, their sacrifice, to the Lord.

14. See Richard C. Edgley, "The Rescue for Real Growth," *Ensign,* May 2012, 52; David F. Evans, "Was It Worth It?" *Ensign,* May 2012, 106; Boyd K. Packer, "Priesthood Power in the Home," Worldwide Leadership Training Meeting, Feb. 11, 2012, lds.org.

15. Larry E. Morris, "Fast Offerings: A Place for the Second Mile," *Ensign,* Feb. 1979, 23.

16. Kimball, "Welfare Services: The Gospel in Action," *Ensign,* Nov. 1977, 79.

17. Ibid.

18. Sacrifice brings forth all kinds of blessings, including better family relationships; an increased ability to love, to repent, to forgive; an increased seeking and understanding of the truths of the gospel; increased health or guidance to healthcare professionals. And sometimes sacrifice brings forth financial blessings. Especially when a prophet of God has promised it will be so.

19. Henry B. Eyring, "Where Is the Pavilion?" *Ensign,* Nov. 2012, 73.

20. See Neal A. Maxwell, "'Swallowed Up in the Will of the Father,'" *Ensign,* Nov. 1995, 22–24.

21. One woman said, "You never miss what you give to the Lord!" That

includes time. So, if you have a huge project to do and you are running out of time to complete it, go to the temple.

22. Russell M. Nelson, "The Sabbath Is a Delight," *Ensign*, May 2015, 131.

23. "Do What Is Right," *Hymns of the Church of Jesus Christ of Latter-day Saints* (1985), no. 237.

24. Quoted in *Nauvoo Relief Society Minute Book*, Apr. 28, 1842, 38, josephsmithpapers.org.

25. Holland, "Place No More for the Enemy of My Soul," *Ensign*, May 2010, 45.

26. Jeffrey R. Holland, "The Ministry of Angels," *Ensign*, Nov. 2008, 30.

27. Smith, *Gospel Doctrine* (1986), 435–36.

28. Moroni 7:29–31.

29. See Neal A. Maxwell, "Premortality, a Glorious Reality," *Ensign*, Nov. 1985, 15–18; Neal A. Maxwell, "Meeting the Challenges of Today," Provo, Utah, Oct. 10, 1978, speeches.byu.edu; David B. Haight, "Temples and the Work Therein," *Ensign*, Nov. 1990, 59; Dallin H. Oaks, "The Great Plan of Happiness,'" *Ensign*, Nov. 1993, 72.

30. Job 38:7.

31. See Maxwell, "Premortality, a Glorious Reality," 15–18.

32. Truman G. Madsen, personal communication, 1995.

33. D&C 2:2.

34. Moses 1:39. See Brent L. Top, *The Life Before* (1988), 192.

35. John A. Widtsoe, "The Worth of Souls," *Utah Genealogical and Historical Magazine*, Oct. 1934, 189; emphasis added.

36. President Boyd K. Packer said: "The question may be asked, 'You mean you are out to provide baptism for all who have ever lived?' And the answer is simply, 'Yes.' For we have been commanded to do so" ("The Redemption of the Dead," *Ensign*, Nov. 1975, 97).

37. See Luke 12:44.

38. See Carlfred Broderick, *The Uses of Adversity* (2008), 9.

39. Elder David B. Haight taught: "Saints of all ages have had temples in one form or another. There is evidence that temple worship was customary from Adam to Noah and that after the Flood the holy priesthood was continued; therefore, we have every reason to believe the ordinances of the temple were available to those entitled to receive them" ("Personal Temple Worship," *Ensign*, May 1993, 24;

see also John A. Widtsoe, "Temple Worship," *Utah Genealogical and Historical Quarterly,* Apr. 1921, 52).

40. Said Elder David B. Haight: "The gospel in its fulness was revealed to Adam. . . . [And] faithful members who understand the eternal nature of the gospel—of God's holy purpose to bring to pass the eternal life of man—understand clearly why the history of man seems to revolve around the building and use of temples" ("Personal Temple Worship," 23–24; see also Widtsoe, "Temple Worship," 53–54).

41. See Dale G. Renlund, "Latter-day Saints Keep on Trying," *Ensign,* May 2015, 56–58.

42. Russell M. Nelson, "Counsel for Families of Faith," 42-stake conference prerecorded broadcast, Salt Lake City, Utah, Feb. 17, 2008.

43. Scott, "The Joy of Redeeming the Dead," *Ensign,* Nov. 2012, 95.

44. Ibid.

45. Ibid.

46. Ibid., 94.

47. Ibid., 95.

48. God is indeed a great compensator. I achieved my highest score in Scrabble after setting it aside for two months and spending my previous "Scrabble time" in family history research.

49. Scott, "Joy of Redeeming the Dead," 95.

50. See Holland, "Ministry of Angels," 30–31.

51. See 2 Nephi 27:20.

52. Quentin L. Cook, "Roots and Branches," *Ensign,* May 2014, 47.

53. See Joel 2:28; Acts 2:17.

54. Jeffrey R. Holland, "Testimony," Seminar for New Mission Presidents, Provo, Utah, June 25, 2014.

55. Schindler's efforts during the Holocaust saved the lives of approximately 1,100 Jews. Today, an estimated 8,500 descendants of the *Schindlerjuden* (Schindler Jews) live in Europe, the United States, and Israel.

56. *Must I, behind locked doors, forever wait,*
    While you, who are on earth, procrastinate
    Work which would set me free?
    Must I cry out, unheard, forevermore . . . ?
    (Clara Lewis Jennings, "Set Your Kindred Free," *Relief Society Magazine,* May 1961, 295)

57. Young, *Discourses of Brigham Young,* sel. John A. Widtsoe (1953), 403–4, emphasis added.

58. Hinckley, "'An Humble and a Contrite Heart,'" *Ensign,* Nov. 2000, 89.

59. Boyd K. Packer, *Mine Errand from the Lord* (2008), 196.

60. *Melvin J. Ballard—Crusader for Righteousness* (1966), 133.

61. Russell M. Nelson, "Covenants," *Ensign,* Nov. 2011, 88.

62. Linda K. Burton, "The Power, Joy, and Love of Covenant Keeping," *Ensign,* Nov. 2013, 113; Carole M. Stephens, "We Have Great Reason to Rejoice," *Ensign,* Nov. 2013, 117.

63. See Russell M. Nelson, "The Sabbath Day Is a Delight," *Ensign,* May 2015, 129–32.

64. "Those who struggle with [sin of any kind] may be disappointed in themselves, but the Savior is not disappointed with any who earnestly seek to repent" (Russell M. Nelson, "To Change Minds and Hearts," Training Seminar for Mission Presidents, Salt Lake City, Utah, Feb. 17, 2015).

65. See Ether 12:27.

66. See Robert J. Matthews, "Our Covenants with the Lord," *Ensign,* Dec. 1980, 33–39.

67. President Boyd K. Packer said: "No member of this Church—and that means each one of you—will ever make a serious mistake without first being warned by the promptings of the Holy Ghost" ("How to Survive in Enemy Territory," *New Era,* Apr. 2012, 3).

68. "Timid souls must learn to be brave; overzealous natures must develop patience; rebellious persons must learn to conform; the slothful must become diligent; the spiritually uncultured must be refined; and all must learn self-discipline" (Matthews, "Our Covenants with the Lord," 35; see also Callister, *Infinite Atonement,* 220–49).

69. Holland, "The Laborers in the Vineyard," *Ensign,* May 2012, 33.

70. See 3 Nephi 20:25–26. "If we can immunize our youth by engraving the doctrine in their hearts, we can raise a strain of sin-resistant Saints" (Nelson, "To Change Minds and Hearts").

71. See "Safeguards for Using Technology" and "Missionary Work in the Digital Age," njmm.org.

72. Ephesians 4:14.